A selection from the series
on people and places first
published in the
Gloucestershire Echo

Written and illustrated by

AYLWIN SAMPSON

THORNHILL PRESS, CHELTENHAM

Published by
Thornhill Press
24 Moorend Road
Cheltenham
MCMXC

ISBN 0-946328-28-5

Typeset by
Cheltenham Newspaper Co. Ltd.

Printed by
BILLING & SONS LTD.
WORCESTER

Contents

AROUND CHELTENHAM

FURTHER AFIELD

Acknowledgement

The Author and Publisher wish to record
their thanks to the Gloucestershire Echo for
assistance in the production of this book.

Introduction

In March 1987 a feature first appeared in the Gloucestershire Echo entitled
'Scene by Sampson.' The idea was to portray by words and drawings
something of the character and history of familiar, and unfamiliar, buildings
in Cheltenham. Soon the rich fabric of places beyond the town was
included, and the weekly series received kind comment from many readers.

Now, thanks to the Editor and the Publisher, it has been possible to present
some of the series in a more permanent form.

How right the seventeenth century traveller Celia Fiennes was when she
wrote:

> 'If all persons would spend some of their time in journeys to visit
> their native land and be curious to inform themselves and make
> observation of each place, it would form such an idea of England
> and cure the itch of over-valuing foreign parts.'

A.A.S.

Cheltenham, 1990

THE impressive towered building at the junction of Park Place and the Park has the self-explanatory name Cornerways, thus concealing an intriguing episode in Cheltenham's past. For this was the entrance to the town's zoo.

Opened officially on Queen Victoria's Coronation day, June 28, 1838, the Zoological and Botanical Gardens attracted large crowds who paid a shilling (5p) to see the grand promenade, a lake, a pagoda, plantations and conservatories, and of course the inmates. There were geese, swans, tropical birds, a pair of Golden Eagles, monkeys, a Bramin Bull and a Norway Wolf.

Today the zoo is no more, and Mr. Dawkes' entrance - lodge with its ground floor aviary now houses College students. But the lake and trees remain; the grand promenade too — and it may still be known to some as the Elephant Walk, even if they don't know why!

1

CHELTENHAM is fortunate in having beautiful parks, and Montpellier Gardens must be one of its greatest treasures. The bandstand is surely the finest in the town, particularly valuable since the one in Imperial Square was sold in 1948 for £175 to Bognor Regis.

Dating from about 1895 it has elaborate cast iron panels, a unique system of construction and indeed an unusual history. Its base originally served as stabling for horses, it later housed targets used by the flourishing Archery Club, and during the last war gave shelter for the winch of a barrage balloon.

No less interesting is the building beyond the bandstand. Although the Gym Centre is relatively recent it rests on the base of what was the auditorium for the Open Air Theatre whose stage was between the two towers. Seating was cleverly adapted so that it could be turned round the other way for bandstand concerts.

Perhaps it might have been possible to view the archery as well from there for the targets were set up on the tennis court banks!

MY DRAWING could prompt much writing about Cheltenham's dilemma, for it illustrates how the need to preserve historic character has to allow for change. The new RoyScot House is an example of the problem when classical and modern are married in one building.

There is no denying the appropriateness of the columns, for they are a reminder of an earlier structure here: the Sherborne or Imperial Spa, which was itself moved from the end of the Promenade when the Queen's Hotel was built in 1837. That, in turn, was demolished with the coming of the Regal Cinema in 1937. When it, too, closed, as the ABC, in 1981 and suffered the same fate as the Imperial Spa four years later, there was much agonising over the design of its successor. The result we see today.

It is good to know that something of the past has remained: there are three of the cinema's decorative plaster plaques made by H. H. Martyns to adorn the new interior. Like the fable of the oak and the reed, my drawing also points out that often mighty buildings fall whereas minor ones survive. Thatchers tea and coffee shop on the right has always been merely an extension of one of the Promenade properties, albeit a delightful little eccentricity.

Once a pastrycook's, then a bookshop, it was indeed demolished, too, but rebuilt in replica, though interestingly change there had to be — not in appearance but in position.

For the whole building was moved four feet to the south!

3

IT IS now more than 40 years since Imperial Gardens lost its 'crystal palace.' Constructed in 1878, Cheltenham's Winter Gardens did not survive the last war. Some said the glass roof was a potential landmark for enemy bombers but it is more probable its demolition was the consequence of neglect following years of disappointment. For, in truth, the building had been something of a white elephant.

At first there were high hopes that here would be great concerts, exhibitions and grand occasions. But expectations were not matched by experience. Proprietors changed with alarming frequency, so, in 1895 the council bought it and put it to such uses as auctions, circuses and roller skating. For a while it served as a warehouse for the Gloster Aircraft Company and as a cinema, though its high dome was hardly suitable, and, in 1935, a theatre was made in its north wing. By 1938, the Winter Gardens were unsafe so, in the early 1940s, the end came and the great glass house was no more.

Yet, strangely, it did not disappear without trace. If you study the path on the east side of Imperial Gardens you will see it curves in an arc; this brought carriages to the entrance. And on the west side, the path past the pond led to the Winter Gardens' other entrance.

Even more interesting, the present tea bar has as its core one of the towers: to the side, looking towards the town hall door, you can see the original brickwork of the north tower. The Skillicorne Garden brickwork also may offer food for thought.

No, the Winter Gardens have not gone.

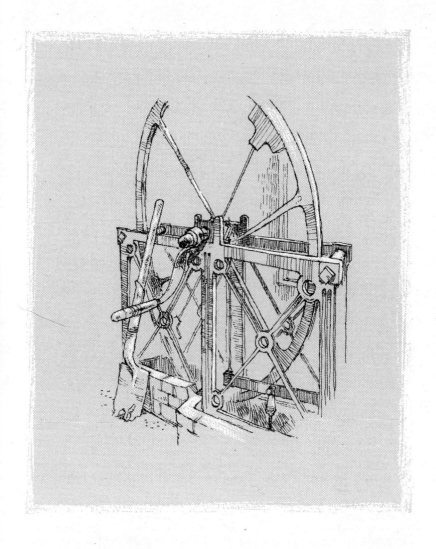

WHEN Buckman wrote his Guide to Pittville in 1822 he recalled that near the site of the Pump Room there was a well whose water had a pleasant saline taste. And that in his younger days he and his companions would 'take a summer ramble through the fields leading to the well, provided with a small jug and armed with a long string.'

That well has gone but beneath the Pump Room can still be seen the successors of that jug and string, namely the original pumps. One is now but a handle but the other, shown in the drawing, has its wheel and beam. Indeed, the wells, too, are there — fearsome shafts with water many feet below.

Buckman would need a very long piece of string for them!

5

ON MONDAY, July 10, 1826, readers of the 'Cheltenham Journal' were treated to a scandal: a handsome young architect had eloped with the only daughter of a wealthy gentleman recently returned from the East Indies! Two weeks later the Journal reported the marriage in London of Edward Jenkins and Charlotte Balfour. Here, surely, is material for a Cheltenham romantic novel.

The architect, Jenkins, had been commissioned to design the church in Suffolk Square but his work was criticised by the authorities who feared structural weakness and, consequently, the more famous J. B. Papworth was called in to complete St. James's. The young lady lived nearby, her father having bought his building plot from James Fisher, developer of much of the Suffolk Square area. Indeed, it is likely Walter Balfour asked Jenkins to design his new house.

That house, from which doubtless the elopement started, still stands. Like Charlotte, it has changed its name, from Southwood to Burlington. The road, too, has changed, for originally it was part of Painswick Road and the row of houses was known as Suffolk Lawn. Today it is familiar as Lypiatt Road. During the first world war the house served as a soldiers' hospital, treating some 1,368 cases, so it is appropriate that its present use is as offices of the Health Authority.

But how strange that it has managed to retain the original railings and gates; all the others in Lypiatt Road have long since disappeared.

6

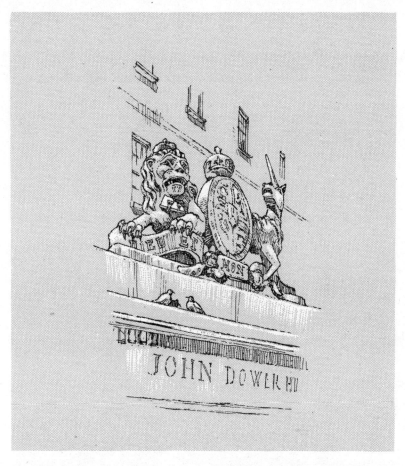

IN 1827 Richard Liddell was a proud landlord, because the Duchess of Clarence had stayed at his boarding house. So what better than to commemorate this illustrious occasion by changing the name of his establishment to The Clarence Hotel, and putting over the porch a fine coat of arms.

Since the Duchess was to become Queen Adelaide a few years later when her husband ascended the throne as William IV, it is hardly surprising to find that the coat of arms is virtually indistinguishable from the King's. When the building was bought by the county authorities in 1858 for a magistrates' office and police barracks the coat-of-arms stayed, giving doubtless appropriate gravity, even if it was out of date.

And when in 1974 it became the headquarters of the Countryside Commission the arms remained as a reminder of Cheltenham's past association with royalty. The man, John Dower, after whom the house is now named, was eminent too, but in a different sphere of history — that of the National Parks movement.

Queen Adelaide would have been pleased, for had not her husband lived the life of a country gentleman for more than fifty years?

7

THERE are few reminders for customers of Sharpe and Fisher in Gloucester Road, Cheltenham, that where now are bricks, timber, glass and all the wide range of builders' supplies, activity of a very different kind took place. Here in fact was a railway station, opened in 1906 as part of the Cheltenham to Honeybourne line.

From 1908 passenger trains used its 700ft. platform and, although as a wartime economy measure it was closed from 1917 to 1919, its value to the town increased so that by 1925 its name was enlarged to 'Cheltenham Spa (Malvern Road).' However, times changed and 1966 saw its last trains. Soon people forgot there had ever been a station there, but clues can still be found. The entrance gates still bear the intertwined letters GWR.

And in my drawing the furthest gabled building has an interior of cast-iron columns supporting a fine braced roof, still much as it was when an engine shed. Beyond can be seen the pinnacles of Christchurch, next to which lived the Rev. Francis Close, who in 1846 protested against Sunday trains, calling them 'a national sin.'

Well, he might now rest content in the knowledge that retribution has been exacted on Malvern-road station!

IN THE early 19th century, one of Cheltenham's prominent persons was the lawyer Thomas Henney. He developed the Promenade and Imperial Spa where the Queen's Hotel now stands. But he was interested, too, in smaller scale additions to the town, for in 1826 he erected 'a curious playing fountain cut out of the purest marble.'

There was a claim that it had been part of the French army's spoils in Italy, coming to England through the interception of a Bristol privateer. Whatever the explanation, it became known as the 'Napoleon fountain.' In 1834 Montpellier Gardens had it as a feature, and there it stayed, gradually decaying and becoming lost in the foliage. However, in 1903 it was rescued, repaired and placed in the Town Hall lobby. Some 23 years later another home was found for it in the vestibule of the public library, but by 1964 it was languishing in the storeroom of the Museum.

Then in 1986 its wanderings ended when it returned to Montpellier. To see it you will have to go into Lloyds Bank — and even then it is not all there, for you may notice that the swan's beak is missing. Tradition says the French soldiers replaced it with an eagle's!

9

AMONG the humble unpretentious terraces of St. Paul's Road it stands like a stranded whale; its arched windows, double-pitched roof and strange angle to the street catch the eye. Originally it was called, somewhat inappropriately, Woodbine Cottage, but when the Irish Lord Dunalley took it he renamed it North Lodge. Inevitably, it ended up being known as Dunalley Lodge or House.

The house, with its elegant bow windows, occupies a site that witnessed not many years before its building a grim episode in Cheltenham's history. For, in 1777, a body was brought here to be hung in chains. A year later, the gibbet and its corpse were torn down, both mysteriously disappearing.

When some time afterwards a hedge was being planted at the spot, the remains were revealed — so frightening the discoverer that he died a few days later.

And if you want to know more about the original crime, look under the rose window inside St. Mary's church where a memorial to Katherine a'Court tells all!

10

WHEN George Rowe published his 'Illustrated Cheltenham Guide' in 1845, he described the Synagogue as 'neat and appropriate' but regretted that the building was not seen to advantage because of its 'retired situation'.

One wonders how many townsfolk today know of its existence, for it is still largely unnoticed and if it were not for the unusual glass roof-light there might be no reason for the passer-by to give its simple facade a second look. Yet here is an important piece of Cheltenham's history. It was in 1834 that the Jewish community bought for £110 a plot of land off St. James's square from John Packwood, commissioned Mr. W. H. Knight to design, and Mr. Hastings to build, a synagogue in the classical style — all for £1,500.

Unassuming the exterior may be, but the inside is a marvellous contrast. Here are furnishings fit for a country house, woodwork worthy of London — and that indeed is the truth, for this interior came from a synagogue in the capital's Leadenhall street.

AT THE end of Montpellier Villas stands the Beehive Inn, its facade displaying an appropriate motto 'By industry we live' underneath a model hive. The industrious John Forbes, architect of St. Paul's Church and Pittville Pump Room, was its designer, as in fact he was for his own house, No. 31, in the street.

But it became the end of the road for him in October 1834 when he was arrested on a charge of forging bills, taken from here to Gloucester and sentenced to transportation. Maybe the symbols on the Beehive name panel were a reminder for him of the foundation stone laying of the Pump Room with full masonic ceremony.

They are still there, as is the street nameplate with its mis-spelling!

IT IS a solid four-square building. You would hardly give a second glance: its gable end has lost its decoration, the panel is crumbling, and the long windows seem to deny any light. Even its porch has gone.

At one time a sorting office, later it hummed with printing presses. But almost 160 years ago, its 60ft room echoed to the voices of children. For this was St. James's Square Infants School, the brainchild, you might say, of that educational pioneer Samuel Wilderspin and the Rev. Francis Close who himself raised £1,200 for its building.

Thus it is the oldest surviving infants school in the country, and its playground one of the first to have swings and climbing apparatus.

No wonder it allowed the public in for an hour each day, 'to observe', in the ponderous words of George Rowe, 'the avidity with which the youthful scholars imbibe the doctrines which will enable them to weather the storms of life.'

ONE of the pleasurable as well as instructive rewards of walking through Pittville is to see the houses on the east side of Pittville Lawn: uniform terraces alternating with detached villas designed to individual's taste.

One of the finest in the classical style is Dorset Villa, built about 1840 by Edward Billings who sold it for £2,800 to Andrew Ramsay. Later occupiers included the family of General Whinyates and one assumes none of them infringed Joseph Pitt's 1827 regulations 'not to carry on any manufactory or any other trade than that of librarian, or hotel or coffee house keeper, or Nurseryman or Florist.'

Today, Dorset Villa houses its largest 'family' of all: students of the Skukutoku College, young ladies from Japan who come to learn something of this country.

Are they told that two of the windows on the elegant south front are a deception, the glass and blinds being backed inside by a brick wall, or that those massive classical columns are in reality hollow from top to bottom?

ONE of the glories of Cheltenham has been its ironwork on balconies or in railings. The name of William Letheren has a prominent place in this aspect of the town, for he and his numerous children were responsible for many fine examples.

His firm too produced the beautiful screen and font canopy in All Saints Church, the gates for Arle Court, the Town Hall's main stair balusters, as well as work in Florence, Bombay and Shanghai. But the most personal must be the gates outside Doric House, Church Road, St. Mark's, for this was William's own house where he lived for over thirty years, though in his time it had the unimaginative name of Suburban Villa.

Let us hope that their elaborate workmanship was some consolation to him as he died brokenhearted in 1910, having seen his firm collapse through his sons' mismanagement.

IN 1816 a blacksmith bought a plot of land described as 'being approximate to Oxstalls Lane near the bridge over the Chelt.' There he built a cottage and called it the Woodlands. Sounds quite pastoral and rustic, doesn't it?

Today we know Oxstalls as Imperial Lane. The Chelt now flows underground at this spot and the Woodlands is Horsley's estate office on Rodney Road, which incidentally used to be Engine House Lane. By 1890 a photographer called Parsons lived there. The house had been deepened, as the join in the brickwork shows, with delightful curved-top windows inserted, while the lattice ironwork of porch, and elegant doorway proclaimed this no ordinary cottage.

If you look at the back you can still see the roof line of Mr. Parsons' studio. For almost 80 years the house remained in the family, till in 1969, when Miss J. M. Parsons died, Horsleys acquired it. Hardly surprisingly, they spent eight times what they paid for it. The floors were riddled with woodworm. The walls merely rested on clay, without foundations. Still, they did discover an extra room under the porch that had been papered over.

Today it looks in apple pie order — and to think that in the 1966 Cheltenham Town Plan a multi-storey car park was intended on this spot!

CHELTENHAM can count itself fortunate to have so characterful a theatre as the Everyman in the centre of the town. Designed by Frank Matcham, architect of such London theatres as the Palladium and Coliseum, the grand opening in October 1891 was a performance by the famous Lily Langtry and her company from the Princess's Theatre, London.

Many great names have been billed here since then: Ellen Terry, Frank Benson, George Robey, John Gielgud, Margot Fonteyn and Robert Helpmann are representative of the varied presentations ranging from ballet to knockabout comedy. How appropriate therefore that its orginal name should have been 'The New Theatre and Opera House.'

Its centrepiece is undoubtedly the auditorium, splendid in carving and colour, classical exuberance and glittering detail combining to present a setting that has been described as one of the finest in the country.

And that by no less an authority than Cheltenham's own actor son, the late Sir Ralph Richardson.

THERE CAN be few buildings in Cheltenham that have no windows fronting the road. You will find one in Christchurch Road, but far and away the most impressive is the Masonic Hall in Portland Street. Here is a truly monumental facade, forbidding and, apart from carved symbols high up, almost anonymous. Its history is worth telling.

In 1817 Foundation Lodge, dating from 1753, came via Abingdon from London. At first it met at Sheldons Hotel in the High Street, then soon decided to buy for £600 a site at the corner of Albion and Portland Streets. The Hall, opened in 1823, was designed by G. A. Underwood, a pupil of Sir John Soane, architect of the Bank of England.

If the exterior is austere, the inside is a complete contrast with its rich world of symbolism. The core of the building is The Temple which has had no expense spared either when it was fitted out or at its restoration in 1982. Its decoration can only be described as magnificent — woodwork, gilding, furniture all ablaze with carving and colour. Other rooms are no less sumptuous. In one, a museum of the Craft has treasures in all forms including an intriguing and rare biographical portrait, recounting through a literal 'word picture' the life of Augustus Frederick, Duke of Sussex. He was a son of George III, one of the Royal Family which came to Cheltenham in that momentous year, 1788.

Today over 10 lodges meet there, and numerous boards recording past officers can be found in The Temple. Some of Cheltenham's illustrious names are on them: men like Baron de Ferrieres, benefactor and mayor, or Henry Boisragon, friend of Dr. Edward Jenner, and himself a physician in the town for 40 years. Incidentally, how strange that Underwood, also a Mason, should have included, against all the rules, windows in the Temple, above the organ gallery. So they have to be kept heavily curtained, and if you look above the neighbouring house in Portland Street you can see 'Underwood's mistakes' on the north wall.

EVEN the most fervent admirer of Cheltenham's architecture would be unlikely to heap praise on the shops in Bath Road. Certainly they are useful and varied, but hardly a tourist attraction. Yet almost hidden among them, and unnoticed by even local residents, there is a delightful memento of Cheltenham's past.

It can be seen on the east side of the street between two shops. Made of cast iron and triangular in section, its bold lettering informs the traveller of distances to Birdlip, and the Market House in Cheltenham. No doubt the former was an encouragement, for the five miles up and over Leckhampton Hill would have been a long pull for horses; while the latter served as a reminder of how close the town was. The Market House — and there were a a number of them through the centuries — has gone, but the one this milestone refers to is that built in 1822 by Lord Sherborne.

It was in the High Street opposite what is now Bennington Street, so perhaps the plaque on the shop corner there, announcing 'Centre Stone,' is our present day equivalent. Incidentally, the date on the top of the milestone is incomplete!

19

CHELTENHAM many times has seen its buildings pulled down and new ones put in their place. Whether the substitution is always for the better can be argued, for sometimes a worthwhile piece of the town's past has gone for ever. But worse is when the site is lost, as in the case of Pate's almshouse.

In 1578, Richard Pate founded a hospital, or almshouse, for six needy Cheltenham persons aged 60 or over. He built it on land fronting the High Street near Rodney Road, providing a courtyard, chapel, orchard, garden and pasture. For more than 240 years the ordered pattern of life went on there, according to Pate's rules: 'Each person shall have a private chamber and a private garden; twice every day they shall be exercised for one whole hour in hearing divine service; and yearly 40 yards of black frieze be distributed to make them livery gowns.'

Then in 1811 their world fell apart. On questionable principles the site was exchanged for a smaller one in Albion Street. A Mr. Smith snapped up the old one for £250 and promptly resold it for £2,000. One can imagine how they felt about the new building; no orchard, no courtyard, no chapel. However attractive the facade may seem, the situation was, in the words of Goding's History, 'most objectionable.'

Today Pate's Almshouses are almost unnoticed by the traffic in busy Albion Street, but by a strange twist of history the site was previously a billiard room, and now next door there's a snooker club.

EVERYBODY thinks of Cheltenham as a Regency town with classical architecture abounding. But here and there buildings can be seen that are exuberantly gothic in style. One gloriously elaborate example is Oriel Lodge, built in 1823 by Edward Jenkins, the designer of St. James' Church, Suffolk Square, for a Charles Timins who was a ship's captain in the East India Company.

Of its later occupants one of the most interesting was Miss Graham-Clarke, for she reputedly was the favourite aunt of Elizabeth Barrett Browning. However, the Timins family connection persisted, and as late as 1931 Mrs. W. J. Haslam, who sold the property to the General Accident Insurance Co., was the great granddaughter of Captain Charles. Interesting as the building's story is, even more intriguing is the tradition that the captain planted a cutting here of a weeping willow tree that grew beside Napoleon's grave on St. Helena.

Indeed, he seems to have distributed several other cuttings in Cheltenham; one was put by the Neptune Fountain in the Promenade, another at the Lypiatts on Lansdown Road. Sadly these have disappeared, but one wonders if somewhere in the town there may still be a surviving reminder of Bonaparte.

It would be appropriate bearing in mind Wellington's association here.

21

SOME SAY it was built by a colonel for his daughter's twenty-first birthday celebrations; others tell a more raffish version and assert that he built it to satisfy his mistress' passion for dancing. Certainly it has all the elegance of a Regency ballroom and its position between Bayshill and Montpellier was ideal for either purpose.

However, perhaps we should take note of an advertisement that appeared in a local newspaper on 3 August, 1867. A Miss Saunders, having bought from Mr. Lea the next door house known as Pierreville, announced 'the reassembling of her classes for dancing and calisthenics at her new residence where she has had a spacious room built and fitted up with all the most medically approved and carefully chosen exercises from the best establishments in England, France and Germany.'

Well, I know which story I prefer. Miss Sayer followed Miss Saunders and in 1926 Miss Gertrude Matthews was running what had by then become known as the Pierreville School of Dancing. Later it declined and the neighbouring grocery shop of Fildes used it as a storeroom. But at least there was nearby a teacher of stage elocution who incidentally included Diana Dors among her clients.

Today the ballroom once again sees the glitter of fashionable clothes even if the music has ceased.

ALTHOUGH traditionally Cheltenham has been noted for its Army connections, the Senior Service must not be forgotten: it also has had its personalities. One example stands out with Duncan Gordon Boyes. He was born in Cheltenham on 5 November 1846 and went to Cheltenham College before joining the Royal Navy.

In September 1864, as midshipman on HMS Euryalus, he was part of a landing party at Shimonoseki Straits, Japan, trying to quell Samurai chieftains who had closed it to shipping. For carrying the Queen's Colour under intense fire, he was awarded the Victoria Cross — at 17½ one of the youngest recipients. On returning to England, the C-in-C Portsmouth presented him with the decoration at a special parade on Southsea Common, witnessed by captains, commanders, sailors and marines, all in full dress uniform, as well as thousands of spectators; while HMS Victory fired a salute.

Tragically, the rest of his life was short and sad. Court martialled for entering the Naval yard, Bermuda, after 11.00 p.m. without a pass, he was dismissed the Service and committed suicide in Dunedin, New Zealand, aged only 23. His home in Cheltenham at 118 Bath Road, known originally as Paragon Buildings, was indeed 'fit for heroes', for his sister Louisa married a lieutenant who also won the VC.

Moreover, even if Duncan Boyes was not to reach high naval rank, another in the family did: Rear Admiral Sir George Boyes, a veteran of the Crimean War, too, lived in this house.

IF YOU walk along Queens Road from Lansdown, you may notice some dignified villas on the right hand side whose doorways are quite extraordinary. One has elaborate vases carved on the surround, another has dolphins. There's a boy stealing bird's eggs from a nest. Fascinating as these six houses are, they serve as merely a prelude to the magnificence of 'Normanhurst', the subject of this drawing.

There, not so far away in Christchurch Road, you will see similar carving but it is all on a larger scale. Normanhurst's bay windows have vases too, each of the eight different; then there are birds — eagle, owl and the familiar by now popinjay — one bird is being attacked by a lizard, or is it the other way round? Lions' heads, gargoyles, a jack-in-the-green, sun rays abound. Indeed, everywhere you look on the facade some fresh detail catches your attention.

Strange that this extraordinary house should have been built by a family with the very ordinary name of Smith. Hannah Smith bought the land in 1882, and Arthur Heavens Smith was the first occupier.

Then, in 1891, Henry Hodgkins of Faringdon acquired it, making it over to his nephew as a 'gift of love'.

But perhaps the most colourful occupier was the formidable magistrate, Stella Louise Ingram, who lived here from 1933 to 1979. How suitable such a residence — Cheltenham's nearest thing to a French chateau!

GO INTO any office where there are framed prints of old Cheltenham and the likelihood is that they will be lithographs by George Rowe. Although not a native of the town, Rowe must be considered the best source of knowing what Cheltenham looked like in the early 19th century. He produced many views in and around the town, caricatures of local personalities and, perhaps most important, a guide in 1845 which illustrated shop fronts, hotels, chapels, houses, streets and parks.

Rowe played a major part in the town's affairs, too, being amongst other things churchwarden of St. Mary's, vice-president of the Horticultural Society, a Town Commissioner, founder member of the Liberal Association, co-owner of the Royal Old Well, a founder of the 'Cheltenham Examiner' and virtually mayor when he became High Bailiff of the Manor of Cheltenham.

However, all that came to a sad end in 1852 with financial ruin. Yet Rowe was not downcast, but courageously emigrated at the age of 56 to seek his fortune in Australia's gold fields. During the 20 years he lived in Cheltenham, Rowe had a number of homes; of them, Exeter House, 60 Grosvenor Street, survives at the end of an imposing terrace.

Why 'Exeter' House? Well, that was where the Rowe family came from and where they returned.

THERE ARE 32 of them in Montpellier Walk: armless ladies whose heads have to take the weight of the beams of shopfront or bank. An initial glance may suggest all to be identical, as uniform as any chorus line. Yet like most first impressions the subsequent truth turns out to be less than plain or simple.

For a start, only two are original in the fact of being made of terracotta by the London sculptor, Rossi, in 1840. The rest are either of stone, carved by Brown of Tivoli Street, or of concrete. Then, one lady is missing. She is now in the Museum having served as the model for the two concrete copies placed on the extension of the NatWest bank in 1970. Of course, the real original ladies are far away, in Athens, carrying out their duty of supporting a porch of the Erechtheion on the Acropolis.

There are only six of them, having their left knee forward — a kind of classical hokey-cokey that went wrong? And there's another intriguing question posed by Montpellier Walk: my drawing shows the north end where the oldest caryatids, as these figures are called, may be found.

Why is King Edward VII also here amongst the ladies? You will see him over the doorway of what is known as Hanover House.

Remembering his statue at the other end of the Walk perhaps these caryatids are really ladies-in-waiting?

IN 1845, Mr. Kirtland had a shop in Pittville Street, being described by Rowe in his guide as a carver, gilder, picture frame and looking glass-maker. His business was followed by that of Harry Rawlings bookseller, Sharpe & Fisher builders, and eventually the present building society Nationwide Anglia.

Fortunately the facade, give or take a cornice and some ironwork, has been preserved over these 150 years, but what we will regret is that the once nearby theatre, a converted malthouse, has gone.

For there in 1774 one of the David Garrick's 'talent scouts' saw a young lady acting, reported back to the great actor and soon she was well set on her road to fame. Her name? Sarah Siddons.

LIKE MANY of its neighbours in Tivoli Road, Cheltenham, No. 35 is a dignified house, the classical proportions proclaiming its early 19th century origin. For some years it was a hotel but now, once again, it is a private house. Not so long ago it earned itself a place in the record books of the police. In 1959 two men had lodgings here and in that year decided to rob Cavendish House.

On the night of October 1st they broke in, having taken the precaution of putting their socks over their hands so as to leave no fingerprints. But one stepped on a fragment of the broken window glass. When the police subsequently raided No. 35, they not only found the stolen goods but also, more conclusively, were able to match toe prints with those on the glass. Thus a conviction was made for the first time on the evidence of footprints.

Who says nothing much happens in Tivoli Road!

ROTUNDA TERRACE in Montpellier Street is one of Cheltenham's most dignified row of shops, standing where there was the Old Well Lane and before that two fields called Skey's Piece.

My drawing shows No. 12, typical of William Swain's development of 1846. In many ways its history is unexceptional: owners like Mrs. Tandy, Mrs. Creese, Mrs. Hailing and Mrs. Margrett; uses like a Post Office, art gallery and now a chemist's.

Yet it has its links with the famous too. For it was here that Cheltenham-born John Nevil Maskelyne worked as a watchmaker, and if a spiritualist's table rapper had not needed repair at his hands, then young John would probably never have gone along to Jessop's Gardens in St. James' Square to scrutinise a display of illusions, and Cheltenham would have lost the opportunity of putting up a plaque to one of the world's great magicians.

SINCE 1891 Promenade House has been the home of the 'Gloucestershire Echo' although the newspaper began in 1873 as the 'Express Telegram'. The founder of the business was S. H. Brookes who declared in the opening issue that if it did not pay it would be dropped, but if encouragement were given then "no effort would be spared in producing a paper of greater pretensions." Well, the years have shown which way it was received.

Promenade House has seen changes in printing technology which would have amazed its previous occupier, Mr. Hale, who had here his Pianoforte, Harp and Music Rooms. Not that he didn't have his achievements too, for at one time the porch proudly bore the Royal Arms as "suppliers to HM Queen Victoria".

However, Promenade House today means the 'Echo', and it is perhaps appropriate to apply to this series another of Mr. Brookes' observations in October 1873: 'We trust that our little venture may possess the qualification of 'multum in parvo' and will be acceptable to the town generally.'

THE NEW extensions, whatever we think of their design, will inevitably divert attention from the original front of Cheltenham's General Hospital. That would be a pity, for the classical grandeur of its portico is a worthy symbol of the town's fine record of medical care.

It began in 1813 with a Dispensary and Casualty Ward in the High Street, providing free advice to the poor. Twenty six years later the hospital moved to Segrave House, later called Idmiston House, and in 1846 to Sandford Road.

What brings such credit to these events is the way the townsfolk responded to the need. Over £2,600 was raised to provide 90 beds by the time the Sandford Road premises opened in April 1849. It would be nice to know that the patients were well looked after too: their diet was potatoes, bread, meat, gruel and beer; and their linen would have been changed fortnightly.

The régime was somewhat strict. One house surgeon made all his patients stand at the foot of their beds, military fashion, when he conducted his ward rounds!

THE BATTLE of Alma on September 20, 1854, was not one of Britain's greatest victories in the Crimean War, but it has given its name to one of Cheltenham's most magnificent houses. Or to be more precise, magnificent interiors. Here are to be seen elaborate classical columns, ornamental detail, gold paint in profusion, and an entrance hall whose grand staircase would not be out of place in the most dignified London club.

Among all this Grecian richness there is another style, that of art nouveau: a copper hooded fireplace beneath a fanciful romantic idyll of pastoral langour, daisy-chain making and pipe playing. Some of the doors have coloured glass or swags that could have come from an elegant Edwardian restaurant or luxury ocean liner.

So it is not surprising to learn that Cheltenham's famous craftsmen of H. H. Martyns were responsible, though the actual designer was a Glaswegian, George Walton, who in 1888 gave up his job as a bank clerk to start a firm of 'Ecclesiastical and House Decorators' on the strength of being asked to refurbish Miss Cranston's Glasgow Tea Rooms. It all fits, doesn't it?

Alma House dates from 1835, the first owner being Admiral Watts. In 1878 the army — and dentistry — took over, with Lt. Col James Clayhills of the 7th Royal Fusiliers, who sold to Richard Rogers, dentist and colonel in the Volunteers. He sold in 1903 to another dentist, George Peake, who apparently held the rank of Lt.-Col. in the Royal Engineers! His widow survived him by only one month in 1944 and the house passed into the possession of the Gloucestershire Dairy & Creamery Co. It was let to Ogdens, the accountants, then to Wheelers Fish Restaurant, and lastly to the publishers of 'This England' magazine.

Not an unimpressive record, and it looks good for another 150 years active service in Rodney Road — also a name redolent of naval action.

WHEN J. R. Scott died in 1831, Thirlestaine House, on which he had spent £80,000, was still unfinished. Nevertheless, the sale brochure described the surroundings like this: 'Gardens and pleasure grounds are laid out with singular taste; they will be found resplendent in American and all plants that are rare and curious.'

'The conservatory and grape house are 42ft. long, the kitchen garden is walled round and there is a carriage drive from the two lodges.' The house's subsequent history is well-known: that Lord Northwick bought it, adding the wings to display his 1,500 paintings, and after him that great eccentric, Sir Thomas Phillips. Then in 1947 Cheltenham College acquired it for £31,000.

Although the pleasure gardens of that 1831 sale have largely gone, there is still one little structure that may serve as a reminder. It stands at the corner of Kew Place, formerly known as Clare Parade, and is like a toy castle. On the old plans it was clearly part of that walled kitchen garden. But one wonders if Sir Thomas Phillips used it to store some of the 100,000 books or 60,000 manuscripts he had amassed.

Whatever its use in the past, its future will be very different, for plans are being made to convert it into an observatory for College pupils.

CHELTENHAM'S Promenade is lined today by prestigious shops and offices but it must not be forgotten that many of them began as private houses or hotels. One of the finest buildings that has undergone changes stands on the west side opposite Cavendish House. It was started in 1823 for a portrait painter called Millet who was said to be 'the only artist successful in discovering the process and vehicle by which Titian and other celebrated masters of the old Venetian school conveyed their colours to the canvas.' A bold claim indeed.

Soon it became celebrated as the Imperial Hotel and in 1856 another change took place when it offered hospitality to 'resident noblemen and gentlemen' as the Imperial Club, admission to membership being exercised with the 'greatest vigilance.' Interestingly, it is recorded that at this time neighbouring small apartments were available for what were termed 'fashionable young ladies'!

However, within 20 years a more prosaic role followed when it became the town's main Post Office and, in 1904, balcony, entrance steps and lamp standards were swept away to allow an extension in heavy classical style to be added to the front.

Then 1987 saw yet another change, to a shop. The whole building has been renovated, the decorative details refurbished, with the pleasing result of a return to 'elegance in the most fashionable and cheerful part of Cheltenham', as an early guidebook put it.

ON JUNE 30, 1841, Samuel Martin moved from 401 High Street in Cheltenham to 4 and 5 Imperial Circus at the Colonnade on a 12-year lease. Soon his son joined the business, and together with a French partner, the name of the clockmakers and jewellers firm became Martin, Baskett and Martin. A branch was opened in Paris too.

That lease also expanded; in the 1850's the shop front could proudly proclaim 'by Royal Appointment,' and although in 1890 a jeweller from Portsmouth, George Dimmer, bought up the concern, the name of Martin continued. Today the great-grandsons are directors; sometimes French clocks bearing the original makers names come in for repair; and even the occasional letter or parcel arrives bearing the old address of Imperial Circus.

The shop may have lost its iron balconies, but, as my drawing shows, much of the facade is unchanged. Inside, on its delightful plaster frieze, cherubs still drink from the wine vat or fight at the grape harvest.

What has changed though is the Circus: now there are motorcycles where once Bristol Blue charabancs used to pull up.

FOR over 70 years Cheltenham Bowling Club has played in Suffolk Square, on what had been George and Annie Shaw's market garden called Home Field, and originally part of Gallipot Farm. The club, founded in 1883, had become somewhat dissatisfied with the public greens in Imperial Square. Thanks to the generosity of Colonel J. T. Ashburner, it was able to move to its new surroundings in 1917, and by 1922 it found itself the proud possessor of two excellent greens together with a delightfully rustic thatched pavilion.

It would have been hard to imagine a finer situation in Cheltenham, for Suffolk Square has some of the most impressive architecture in the town. My drawing shows but one part of the north side and of that, Willoughby, the end house in a magnificent terrace. Built in 1824 for William Richardson, it changed hands in 1903 for £800, passing to Mr. and Mrs. Millington who bred Jack Russell terriers for hunting. From 1923 to 1963 it was divided up as flats before becoming a hotel.

Throughout its history, Willoughby has welcomed visitors. Back in the early years when it was the only house on that side of the square fashionable society stayed there. In 1837 we learn that the family of the Earl of Moray had been in residence three or four years, while ten years earlier no less a person than the Duke of Gloucester, cousin to the Prince Regent and the Duke of Suffolk chose it for his annual visit to Cheltenham. It was to this address that the future Queen Adelaide came to dine with him in the July of that year.

Which makes one wonder if the coat of arms on the Countryside Commission's John Dower House, put up after she had stayed there, should not have had a companion one of the Duke's over Willoughby's porch?

36

NOW, when the Promenade, Cheltenham, is all shops and offices it is worth being reminded that in the past many were private houses. Those on the west side overlooking Imperial Square are particularly impressive and interesting for they have kept much of the character of the houses. In the early years of the last century they looked onto Mr. Hodges Nursery Ground, their backs being bounded by Painswick Road, later known as Old Well Lane.

The subject of my drawing is 121, Promenade, though it was originally called 1, Cambridge Villas. Robert Cope lived in it from 1837 and it remained in that family till 1875 when George Rodger bought it for £1,700. To show that house prices have not always increased, it should be noted that in 1917 Michael Buck, proprietor of the Pierpoint Hotel, paid only £500 for it. In 1945 Agnes Barton went to live as companion to Mr. Buck's widow, and remained there till her death in 1982. Thus ended an era of the Promenade's history, for this was its last private house.

And what a 'time capsule' it proved to be: cast iron gas stoves, a massive coal range in the cellar, period fireplaces, wallpaper and curtains that seemingly had not been changed this century; there was a mahogany seated loo, and, most extraordinary of all, some 80 clocks! Today the structure has been thoroughly overhauled, the original ironwork restored, and the interior refurbished in keeping with the solicitors who own it.

But fortunately it has not been so modernised that one cannot still picture a Mr. Cope or a Mrs. Buck peering through lace curtains to observe who was coming down Promenade Road West.

IN KINGSMEAD Road, Cheltenham, there is one building that stands out from the others, literally head and shoulders above them. Its mellow rich brickwork and elegant porch suggest an age somewhat greater than that of the neighbouring 'semis'. In fact there has been a house on this site since Domesday Book times, for this was where Arle Manor stood. The accompanying church has gone, and indeed most of the manor house was demolished by 1880, but something remains to remind us of the historic spot.

What we see today at Arle Court House is the early 18th century brick front, and behind it a few traces of the medieval structure. The original entrance on the Tewkesbury Road, the last of its gate-houses surviving until 1971, gave on to a tree-lined drive which came up to the west side of the house over a moat fed from the Chelt. Many famous names have been associated with the house including the Lygon family and the Butts. When the present occupants moved in, they discovered a cellar which had been sealed up. It was spotlessly clean, though in the centre of the floor was a decomposing barrel.

This, they found out, was a traditional way of exorcising a ghost. Thankfully, they say, it did not work, for the ghost is still there!

ON June 11, 1931, an aeronautical designer returned home to his flat in Lansdown Terrace, Malvern Road, Cheltenham, to find a telegram awaiting him. It was an enquiry from the Kawasaki Aircraft Company in Japan about a new kind of landing wheel publicised by the inventor a month earlier.

Events from then on moved fast, for the designer's company, Gloster Aircraft, withdrew being unwilling to keep its estimate low enough. Thereupon the designer resolved to produce the wheels himself, resigned from the company and, renting a mews loft in the lane behind his flat, equipped it with a workbench, a manually operated pillar drill and a few hand tools, and set to work.

Despite the neighbouring premises being a petrol store, and the floor below having an abundance of wood shavings, no fire insurance was taken out; the designer asserted he could not wait for the formalities, and anyway he could keep watch from his flat. By September 21, the finished wheels were on their way to Japan. The rest is history as they say.

For that was the beginning of George Dowty's great engineering empire, and there's a plaque on the wall of the mews in Lansdown Terrace Lane to tell us where those six wheels were made.

CINEMAS which have become something else usually lose their character and invariably their name. But in Cheltenham one has kept both.

My drawing is of The Daffodil, itself an unusual name, in Suffolk Parade. It looks virtually the same outside as when it opened in October 1922 with a 'Thunderclap' — the film of course. Inside it was well appointed: a lounge complete with tiled fireplace, paintings and oak panelling; an orchestra pit with brass railings; hanging lights like daffodils and wallpaper bearing motifs strangely like Pitman's shorthand!

What a contrast to the neighbouring shops with their stonework dating from 1846. But perhaps the younger employees of Fred Sims, baker and confectioner welcomed the celebrated double seats in the balcony, bookable in advance at 1s 3d each. Two were displayed in the foyer, doubtless to publicise them to courting couples.

Today they have gone, but the Daffodil still has its surprises: only recently the projection room was discovered, fully equipped even to films.

MOST towns have their Master Builders, but Cheltenham can claim a Mistress Builder, too. She was the Honourable Katherine Monson, daughter of a Lincolnshire baron, and her most spectacular work in the town can be seen as St. Margaret's Terrace. The terrace is almost as impressive from the back — the drawing shows the generous bow — as from the frontage onto St. Margaret's Road.

Not surprisingly, many of Cheltenham's leading families chose to live there; but bankruptcy overtook the Mistress Builder. She fled to France, only returning to the scene of her greatest achievement for the last few years of her life, dying within sight of her Terrace at her clerk of work's house in North Place, in April 1843. Her resting place is also not far away, outside the door of Holy Trinity Church.

Yet perhaps for most townsfolk her name lives on as Monson Avenue.

FOR over a century Cheltenham College Baths have stood by the road to which they gave their name, and, as my drawing shows, little seems to have changed over the years. In 1919 on a wet summer's day, when cricket had been cancelled, the young gentlemen, finding the Baths shut, broke in and threw the keeper, who doubtless emerged from the neighbouring lodge, into the pool.

The next day another attack was thwarted only by the police who warned the Principal that the keeper had reported the matter to his Trade Union. With the likelihood of a reprisal upon the College, the Principal mustered the O.T.C. cadets, and armed with rifles they prepared to repulse a large crowd bearing down on the College.

Mercifully, negotiations began, the Principal promising to flog the offenders and the Union demanding to be present then. However, all ended amicably when, at the appointed hour, the Union representatives, learning that those to be flogged had offered to take the punishment on behalf of everyone else, begged for an amnesty — and the incident was closed.

MY drawing is not of a church but a delightful boathouse which stands in the Park. Its 'steeple' is a miniature dovecot surmounted by an elaborate weathervane, while the water end has a generous arch. It would be nice to think this little gem of wooden architecture has been here since the Park opened in 1838, or even that it is as old as the house which can be glimpsed beyond, but I suspect that Fulwood built in 1847 had so many occupants none would have stayed long enough to enjoy boating.

However, perhaps Mrs. MacKnight-Crawford had it erected when she added the large conservatory to the house at the turn of the century, for I'm sure the nuns who ran the Ursuline Ladies College here from 1913 to 1931 would have had little use for it. In 1931 St. Mary's Training College bought Fulwood, though with the outbreak of war evacuation was ordered. Nevertheless in 1940 the College returned, to be greeted by a bomb which landed as the thirteenth van stood to be unloaded.

Strangely its contents of glass and china escaped without a crack, and although Fulwood's north wing was damaged, the boathouse survived unharmed.

CHELTENHAM'S big public schools are well-known, but no less important are those humbler institutions which can be found around the town,
tucked away in some ordinary street. They are as much part of the fabric of
education as the Ladies' College or Dean Close School; indeed it could be
argued they have a more significant link with Cheltenham's children.

One example is to be found in Devonshire Street. Its gothic windows
seem to echo the majestic facades of Cheltenham College even if its pupils
came from less well-off families. Yet in a way its pedigree is longer than that
of any public school in the town for it was the direct successor of a school
established in 1683 in the room over the north porch of the parish church,
and re-endowed by Lady Capel in 1713. Thanks to the Rev. Francis Close,
it did not disappear when national schools began, but found a new home
here off the High Street.

Maybe life for its pupils was not so colourful as when the churchyard
served as their playground and their aged headmaster, John Garn, had to be
manhandled up the steep stairs to the classroom by early 'pupil power'.

But the poignant War Memorial still to be seen on the outside wall tells of
the contribution such schools have made to town and country.

'They trod of old the fields we tread,
They played the games we play,
The part of them that is not dead
Belongs to us today.'

EVERY town's High Street sees change in its buildings over the years. Shops alter their fronts and we have to look above the plate glass to see traces of the original design. However, Cheltenham is fortunate in having a number that are easily recognisable even after a century of varying use.

One good example is today's C&A shop in the Upper High Street. It began as the County of Gloucester Bank in the early 19th century, being known as 'Pitts Bank'. Apparently it had a financial crisis before many years had passed for in 1825 John Gardner, owner of the town's main brewery and a partner with Joseph Pitt in the bank, had to make a frenzied trip to London to bring back enough money to meet shareholders' demands.

But the bank's finest hour surely came in 1888 when it offered to accept £5,400 if the Corporation would purchase the Pump Room and gardens which Pitt had owned, in part settlement of his death debt of £10,800. So in effect this is the building where Pittville Park was saved for the town. It is said that when the motor firm of H. E. Steel took over the building at the turn of the century conversion was easy in one respect for all that had to be done to the words over the entrance was to substitute 'Garage' for 'Bank'!

It would not have been quite as simple when occupancy changed later to the Gloucestershire and Severnside Co-operative Society.

CHELTENHAM has it share of hauntings and of all its buildings, the one perhaps which has greatest claim to be the best known for its apparition is St. Anne's in Pittville Circus Road. Built in 1860, its owner was a Mr. Henry Swinhoe who degenerated into an alcoholic, and led his second wife, Imogen, the same way. It was after these two had died that the first appearances of a tall woman dressed as a widow were reported.

During the next ten years, when the house was let to the family of Captain Despard, the ghost was seen in many rooms and in the garden where, we are told, the children would form rings round her. By the turn of the century the house was being converted into a private school, but maybe the hauntings continued, for the enterprise did not last many years. Strange therefore that in 1935 St. Anne's became a Church Diocesan Retreat, with a chapel being added in 1962.

Then, eight years later, it was sold to be made into the flats of today. Perhaps the ghost has been frightened off by all these changes!

IT IS strange that Cheltenham, which benefited so much from the visit of George III, should have no statue to him — yet William IV whose chief association with the town was through his wife Adelaide has a fine monument, in Montpellier Gardens, where he stands in his robes of the Order of the Garter.

Nevertheless the people of Cheltenham had reason to be grateful to King William for it was through his personal support that the Reform Bill became law in 1832, thus enabling them to have their own Member of Parliament. And so this statue, the work of a local sculptor, came to be placed in Hodge's Imperial Nursery, now Imperial Gardens.

But when? For on its plinth we are told it was 1833 "to commemorate the passing of the Reform Bill," yet Rowe in his Guidebook gives the occasion as the King's Coronation Day, September 8, 1831. Moreover who paid for it? Again, the plaque tells us it was by public subscription; Rowe says it was Thomas Henney! Anyway at least we can be certain of the date it was moved to its present site, 1920; and when it was restored, 1985 — for, like people, statues can have facelifts.

Perhaps William one day will have a companion in George whose royal visit set the town on its way to fame?

47

THIS is the road that didn't go according to plan; the exception you might say, that proves the rule, for we are so used to seeing Cheltenham's terraces and villas set out with precision and regularity. The story begins in 1835 when Captain William Beetlestone built No. 2, Pittville Lawn as part of a grand terrace to be called Segrave Place West. But that was as far as he got!

When Joseph Pitt himself died in 1842, all the building land between No. 2 and Halsey House on Wellington Road was acquired by the County of Gloucester Bank. A Thomas Cantell bought the frontage, promptly resold it in plots and a carpenter named William Hart had the one next to No. 2. With commendable design sense, he built a matching half to complete the pair, calling it Napier House.

But then problems arose, for the remaining plots were given smaller pairs of houses and although two could be fitted in, there wasn't room for a third. So, once again, a 'half measure' had to be taken. And if you look at the result you'll see that Clarendon Villas, as they were called, had to be tacked on to No's. 2-4!

Still, it made for variety and Cheltenham would be the poorer without these refreshing quirks.

IT WAS a grand idea that the butcher, Joseph Hughes, hatched in the 1820s. He would have a mini-Pittville on the other side of Prestbury Road, with an elegant square, fenced-in and laid out as a garden for the residents.

Around it there would be houses with fine porches and impressive balconies, all contributing to produce what might become 'Hughesville.'

But in 1827 the butcher went bankrupt, his plans were abandoned, and the garden was soon built over. Yet something survived, for the name Portland-square can still be seen, and its east side, though renamed Albert-place in 1843 to honour the Prince Consort, retains some of those fronts butcher Hughes dreamed of.

SHOPPERS busily wheeling their supermarket trolleys along High Street probably give hardly a second glance to the building standing at the corner of St. George's Place. Yet among the plate glass and concrete modernity, this odd gabled shop — or amusement centre, as it is currently designated — has a place in the story of the town.

In 1809 it housed the offices of the Gloucestershire Echo and Chronicle, while six years earlier it had seen the publication of Ruffs 'History of Cheltenham'. So in a way it has been in its time at the centre of news.

Although its subsequent use has included being a pastry cooks', and jeans shop, there is still something about the building that suggests a proud past.

BEAUFORT House stands in Montpellier Terrace, Cheltenham, overlooking the Gardens. Originally the road was to be called South Parade — to echo on the other side of the Gardens North Parade, now Montpellier Spa Road. Built in 1826 it is a fine example of late Regency style with an elegant stone staircase and wrought iron balconies.

For some years it served as a boarding house for Cheltenham College, and so well liked was it by the housemasters that, when it ceased to be used as such, two of them stayed on. But there was also a less attractive episode in the house's history, when it became the Cheltenham headquarters of the British Union of Fascists in the 1930's. Its founder, Sir Oswald Mosley — whose private army had to be disbanded by Act of Parliament — came there to address a rally.

Perhaps it is just as well Montpellier Terrace was not called South Parade then!

THE Churchyard of St. Mary's, Cheltenham's parish church, has today an air of spaciousness but in 1829 the authorities were glad that a small orchard on the south side of Lower High Street had become available for purchase. For the situation, bluntly, was that the churchyard was filling up.

So the orchard was bought, the trees cleared and by 1831 a chapel opened at a cost of £600. When, 30 years later a new cemetery was opened, Lower High Street ceased to echo to the sound of hearses and for almost a century the site was forgotten. Then, in 1966, it began a fresh life as the Winston Churchill Memorial Garden, today its chapel hosts toddlers' playgroups as well as martial arts devotees.

Thomas Letheren's entrance gates, originally at Cyphers Nursery Gardens in Queens Road and worthy successors to those made by the renowned firm of Marshall's, still provide a fleeting glimpse of that classical facade for the hectic traffic streaming along the High Street.

WHEN, around 1800, Robert Hughes built his house, its back garden must have been the longest in Cheltenham, for it stretched from the High Street right the way down to Oriel Terrace by the Chelt. His father, Thomas, had come to the town in 1749, married a wealthy heiress of the Bridges family, and bought Powers Court Estate.

It was on this land that Thomas built in 1784 the lower Assembly Rooms, at the corner of the High Street and Rodney Road, then called Engine House Lane. And it was on this land, too, that Robert's house, to be known as Rodney Lodge, stood, facing the High Street, its beautifully proportioned bay windows looking south down the garden to Woodland Cottage and the bridge. Altogether a property of some distinction befitting a prosperous solicitor and leading Freemason.

How better to describe it than to quote from a sale notice of a few years later: 'Rodney Lodge, lately in the occupation of the Earl of Ailesbury, the Marquis of Ormonde, the Earl of Coventry, and lastly the Conde de Funchal; with the shrubbery ground, fruit garden, stable and meadow containing three acres, a paddock with groups of old forest trees bounded by the Chelt in which there is an ancient Right of Fishery ... altogether a possession not be be equalled in Cheltenham.'

Even allowing for the accepted hyperbole, a pretty impressive offer! Today those grounds have long since been occupied by terraced houses, decently set back so as not to spoil the view from the bow, and the front to the High Street has been blocked by a bank.

However, one distinction remains: it must be the only house in Cheltenham whose side porch straddles the pavement.

53

MELLOW, honey coloured Stanway House in the Cotswolds has seen many famous faces. In this present century when the Earl and Countess of Wemyss lived there such people as G. K. Chesterton, H. G. Wells, Walter de la Mare and even Queen Mary visited it. One, though, has left more than just a memory or a name, for if you take the road around the church, past the garden wall, on the left there is a cricket field and at its edge a delightfully rustic, thatched pavilion. This was given by the author Sir James Barrie.

He was a keen cricketer, and in the year that he paid his first visit to Stanway the Australians were playing at Cheltenham. Not surprisingly Barrie got them invited over on the Sunday, thus starting a tradition of matches against guest elevens. The following year 1922 saw Eton College team there, interestingly including in its players young Nicholas Davies, one of the brothers who inspired Barrie to write 'Peter Pan'.

Three years later he gave the pavilion to Stanway and from then until his death in 1937, Barrie enjoyed seeing his favourite game from its little verandah. Not that he was merely a passive spectator, for there is the story about his meeting with the great cricket writer Neville Cardus at Lords when Barrie apparently said: 'You must come down to Stanway ... I can bowl so slow that if I don't like the ball I can run after it and bring it back!'

FOR 21 years silk printing has flourished at Beckford in the delightful grounds of the former vicarage. A more idyllic place with the medieval church in the background and venerable trees around might be hard to imagine. Yet, as is often the case, history reveals less attractive episodes. Here our story centres on the Rev. John Timbrill who was appointed vicar in 1797, and for the next 68 years held the living, though not the hearts of his parishioners.

For it seems he was not a particularly likeable parson. As a Justice of the Peace he reputedly used his influence to assure a young man from Ashton-under-Hill that it would be better for him to be tried for sheep stealing at Gloucester Assize than by Evesham Bench. The result was that he was hanged, and so incensed were the people of Ashton, that they formed their own Free Church — and it is still there. Beckford's squire Mr. Wakeman also fell out with Timbrill. He decided to build a village wash-house in the grounds of his house next to the vicarage, and put it on stilts so the washerwoman could look into the parson's garden. Timbrill promptly put up a screen — you can see the large iron staples for it on the wall in my drawing.

But there is a more homely reminder of the Timbrill family in the old vicarage itself: signatures of two of his children scratched with a diamond on window panes.

COUNTRYSIDE museums are familiar to many Gloucestershire visitors, and one of the most fascinating is that at Bibury, not only because it has working machinery as well as a delightful hotch-potch of collections ranging from farm implements, Victorian bygones, toys and prams, to furniture owned by the famous hymn writer John Keble, but also because they are all housed in a magnificent 17th century mill.

Most visitors to Bibury want to see Arlington Row, as well as the mill used for fulling the cloths woven in that picturesque group of cottages. It was also a corn mill. Unfortunately in 1914 the original machinery was dismantled for scrap, but when in 1965 restoration took place, replacements came from North Cerney mill. My drawing was done from the writing room of The Swan, an inn that also has welcomed many visitors, among them William Morris and maybe Dean Swift or Alexander Pope.

But, if the following tale be true, there was one visitor the landlord of the time could have done without. It seems that a young Oxford student offered to show mine host how mild ale and strong beer could be drawn from the same cask. He bored a hole in a full one, asking the landlord to plug it with one finger; he then bored another with a similar instruction. On pretence of going to fetch some pegs, the young trickster rode away leaving the landlord a prisoner in his own cellar.

Yet the outcome was to the landlord's benefit, as so many people called to have a laugh at his expense that custom grew beyond all expectation!

THE village of Cowley lies low in the valley of the river Churn, its great
house and medieval church creating a delightful pastoral scene. Yet this
corner of Cotswold tranquility has its links with the world of international
companies, and indeed with eccentricity — for here an 18th century squire
squandered the family fortune in a passion for bell ringing!

However it is with a later owner that we are concerned, and his
tombstone features in my drawing. Here is the resting place of Sir James
Horlick, a pharmacist, who after qualifying in 1869 turned his attention to
formulating the infant food that was patented in America as 'malted milk'.
By 1885 the Horlick's Milk Company was established, and five years later a
London branch opened. By 1945 the British section of the company had
prospered enough to take over the American side. Sadly, Sir James did not
live to see that, for he died in 1921. Nevertheless he has his memorial at
Cowley.

How appropriate that 'Horlick's milk' should be forever associated with a
place which means 'cow pasture', and a river that is called Churn!

IT WAS not until long after Miss Anna Gordon died in 1884 that the Coffee Tavern beside Kemble station was licensed, for Miss Gordon had resolutely respected the wishes of her father, the temperance Member of Parliament Robert Gordon. Furthermore, she was not greatly in favour of the station either, again reflecting father's views.

For it was he who insisted that only employees of the Cheltenham & Great Western Union Railway Company might use it, apart from members of the Gordon family who had the privilege if they gave prior notice to the station master at Cirencester. But then, since the line passed through their 8,000 acres, they assumed a certain entitlement in the matter. However, the Gordons got as they say their come-uppance when a director of the company travelling to one of Lord Bathurst's Hunt Balls at Cirencester had to change trains here.

He did not appreciate waiting in a draughty cold shed in the winter, and so, before many months had gone by, an Act of Parliament had included in its provisions powers for the company to buy land on the Gordon estate. The result was today's delightful station with its cast iron columns entwined with ribbons, and its Tudoresque stonework.

As for that coffee tavern, well it was re-named the 'Station Inn,' and although it again calls itself the "Tavern" somewhat stronger drink than Robert Gordon or Miss Anna would have wished is consumed.

TO ENTER Sapperton church is to be back in the days of Queen Anne. You expect to see the parson in his gown and bands, to hear the village musician's bas viol or serpent sounding from the gallery, and to glimpse deep in the family pew the local squire dozing in his periwig and laced coat. Everywhere is Jacobean carving, dark rich woodwork, scrolls and strapwork. Mind you, close examination does suggest it might be a little out of place: that table in the sanctuary looks uncommonly like a 17th Century sideboard, and, as for those figures on the pew ends, surely they were intended for a different setting?

Yes, as a matter of fact all this came from a house, which Lord Bathurst demolished in 1730. You can see its site just north of the church. Sir Robert Atkyns, senior, had lived there, and his son's memorial fills the south transept. What a splendid affair it is: Sir Robert junior reclines, elbow on pillow, in full wig, loose ruffled sleeves, square toe buckled shoes, and holding a book. The inscription tells us that 'he left behind him his most dear and sorrowing widow who erected this monument to his memory, though he left behind him one more durable, The Ancient and Present State of Gloucestershire'. For the book he holds represents the first history of the county and it is a pity he did not live to see it published in 1712.

Once he engaged in a duel at Perrot's Brook. His adversary, Sir John Guise, one of King William's supporters, came off badly for we are told Sir Robert ran him through, 'the sword going in at his navel and coming out at his backbone, he falling into a sandpit and the sword breaking in his body.'

However, Sir John survived to be fit enough to challenge one of King James's men outside Gloucester cathedral.

59

ONCE upon a time, as all good stories start, a certain Sir Robert Fry was journeying in the Cotswolds when fog descended. Losing his way he wandered blindly, and had given up all hope of finding the right path when through the swirling mist came the sound of a distant bell. Guided by it he eventually arrived at Moreton-in-Marsh, and in gratitude he left money to ensure there would always be a ringer to help other travellers.

Learning that the bell rang at certain times he added another payment for the clock. So until 1860 the bell sounded from the Curfew Tower in Moreton's main street twice daily, at six in the morning and eight at night. But in that year old William Webb who was also town crier, parish sexton, beadle and constable as well as curfew ringer, had his leg broken trying to put a drunk into the tower — for it served also as the town lock-up.

Perhaps the offender had been next door at the Crown Inn (you can still see the name over the door). The accident decided William to call it a day so far as ringing the curfew was concerned, and from then on Moreton lost something of its past. Today the tower and its clock and its bell niche can still be seen, but the bell now only summons the fire brigade.

Strange when, not so far away from this, the oldest building in the town, should stand a sign directing visitors to the Fire Service College.

IN RECENT years the main road from Cheltenham to Stow has been changed, so it is less likely that you will drive through Lower Swell if you are in a hurry. But if time allows take the more leisurely route, and with it the opportunity to look at the group of extraordinary cottages pictured in my drawing. They stand on the northside of the road leading up the hill to Stow. The centre cottage has curving dormer window hoods topped by fir cones, the main windows have honeysuckle decoration, while the front door is shaded by a highly individual canopy ending in a pineapple.

There are further strange windows in the flanking cottages, though they do not have an elaborate carved parapet. Who designed this oddity and why? Well, not far away is another, larger house called Sezincote, and the architect for that Oriental fantasy was Samuel Pepys Cockerell who was architect too for the East India Company as well as the designer of Warren Hastings' new house at Daylesford.

So we can be pretty sure that Cockerell was responsible for these cottages. So why were they built? The answer can be found on a plaque above the westernmost door: spa water 'Carbonate calybeate discovered 1807', and if you miss that, then the name of the centre 'Pineapple Spa Cottage' should help.

Come to think of it, Lower Swell should have celebrated its sesquicentennial (150 years) as a spa in 1957!

THE Shurdington Road has a wide range of architectural styles along it, from modern estate to rustic cottage, but without doubt its most impressive building, set in a park-like landscape, is the Greenway Hotel. Here the Lawrence family had lands as early as 1521, though the 'greenway' from which the hotel takes its name dates back to pre-Roman times when it provided a safe walkway through marsh and forest for the flocks of Cotswold sheep.

The house we see today was begun in 1584, and, although alterations or additions inevitably followed, it is not difficult to identify the original layout. Within the rooms there are delightful furnishings, much Jacobean panelling and two superb fireplaces.

Outside, the lake and dovecot may have disappeared but the majestic trees and yew hedges remain. It was in 1947 that the house became a hotel welcoming visitors from all over the world. Perhaps one of its most memorable was a Prime Minister, for in July 1982 Mrs. Thatcher 'booked in', just for two days.

Rather different from Dulcibella Lawrence — she ruled the house in the 18th century for over 54 years.

THE WAY from the High Street to Chipping Campden's glorious 15th century church and the picturesque almshouses takes you up the road shown in my drawing. It is an attractive scene with the Eight Bells Inn to the left, and old houses everywhere. But the one you should notice is on the right: it is called Perry's Cottage and is a reminder of a bizarre episode in the town's history.

William Harrison, the 70-year-old steward of Lady Juliana, was its chief character. On August 16, 1660, he set off from Campden to collect some of his mistress' rents at Charringworth, three miles away. He disappeared, with only a comb and blood stained neckband found. Suspicion fell on Harrison's servant, John Perry, and despite conflicting stories he, his brother and their mother were hanged for murder on the Broadway Hill gallows.

Two years later, one autumn evening, William Harrison walked into his house alive and well. His account of the intervening time sounded too preposterous for words: kidnapped by horsemen, sold to a ship's captain, captured by Turkish pirates on the high seas, slave to a physician at Smyrna, escape and stowaway to Lisbon, to Dover and so home! What the truth behind his absence was we may never know, but Harrison's wife soon after committed suicide, and the sentencing judge refused to accept that William had returned.

Hardly surprising therefore that the whole affair has been called the 'Campden Wonder' — and if you are curious to see what Lady Juliana looked like find her monument in the Hicks chapel of the parish church.

It is almost as bizarre as the episode.

IF YOU take the London Road out of Cheltenham it is almost certain that, as you pass Dowdeswell Reservoir, your attention will be caught by Rossley Gate, a prominent half-timbered house on the opposite side of the road, set amongst trees and wild flowers. In 1929 this house attracted the attention of Cecil Coxwell Rogers, but then it was in a very different place, namely, at the corner of Arle Avenue and Gloucester Road in Cheltenham where the Infants' school was to be built.

For £500 he had the house taken down and rebuilt at the present spot to serve as a gatehouse to Rossley Manor, a property he had inherited some years before. So now it enjoys a splendid rural view looking across to the lake made in 1886, and sheltered behind by the embankment of the old Banbury to Cheltenham railway — a reminder of its Cheltenham days, for the Gloucester railroad was just across the street then.

How strange that the town's oldest house, dated by some as mid-fifteenth century, should have been preserved only by moving it some miles into the country.

Perhaps threatened buildings in the town today might be saved in a similar way?

YOU couldn't wish for a more distinguished pair of designers for the 18th century church at Croome d'Abitot than Robert Adam and 'Capability' Brown. Yet even their work is overshadowed by the sculptures of Nicholas Stone and Grinling Gibbons. These memorials to the families of the Earls of Coventry include one to Maria, wife of the 6th Earl, whose beauty caused the king to provide soldiers as her bodyguard in Hyde Park, and whose shoemaker in Worcester charged the public for a glimpse of her footwear.

She died aged 27, but we remember her by her Tower at Broadway. The large house in my drawing is of course the Coventrys' home of Croome Court, and clearly Adam as well as Brown had a hand here too. But perhaps even these great names would have been eclipsed if, in our century, others had taken up residence. For during World War II this was to be a refuge for the Royal Family in the event of invasion. However, when boxes labelled 'Buckingham Palace' began arriving, the secret was out, and the plan had to be abandoned.

One last thought: I was told that Queen Mary and her husband George V spent part of their honeymoon here, so perhaps Croome Court had Royalty after all.

THERE is something sad about a deserted mansion with its shuttered windows, echoing stables, overgrown flowergarden and unkempt lawns. Such a place at the moment is Toddington Manor. Admittedly it is not all that old; if you want to see its predecessor, its ruined gateway is next to the church.

But Toddington Manor has the appearance of a medieval palace; there is a magnificent tower, based it is said on that of Magdalen College, Oxford, while its great south window would do justice to Tintern Abbey. Everywhere turrets, pinnacles and battlements give a breathtaking richness. Indeed it comes as no surprise to learn that the designer of all this, Charles Hanbury-Tracy, was chairman of the Selection Committee for the Houses of Parliament competition, and that thanks to him the gothic style of Sir Charles Barry was adopted — or to know that Hanbury-Tracy himself produced an alternative proposal in the same style.

But then his was an extraordinary family. He married his cousin who was descended from King Ethelred the Unready, and from the Tracy who as one of the Four Knights murdered Thomas à Becket.

Not perhaps something to be proud of, so it's odd to find carved each side of Toddington's main door a knight drawing his sword and a prelate losing his mitre.

YOU will find Maugersbury not far from Stow-on-the-Wold, by taking a leafy lane down the hill. It is a delightful hamlet, with picturesque cottages, a manor house dating back to the 16th century, and plenty of clematis, rose and wisteria. All it lacks is a church, though it has another building that is rather more unusual in so small a place.

For here is a crescent of houses which would not look out of the way in Cheltenham. Its centre door has above it a carved crest, giving a clue to the reason for this stranger in the hamlet. For it is Edmund Chamberlayne's. He was lord of the manor and a fine example of a squire who had real concern for his poorer tenants, devising a scheme to house four families in a kind of commune. There was a large central room to be used as a Sunday School, a public oven furnace with coal store underneath, and each tenement had an acre of garden, together with a pig!

Today this crescent, built in 1800, is all that remains of the enterprise, and it too was saved from dereliction only through the energy of an American lady who converted it into a single dwelling.

EVEN when you may be threading your way through traffic at the narrowest part of Winchcombe, there will be no mistaking Jacobean House which at least gives those stuck in the congestion an architecture lesson. Its gables and front door are copybook examples of the changeover from medieval to classical style in the early 17th century.

Here in 1618, the town's King's School found itself in a purpose-built house with a large schoolroom on the ground floor and master's accommodation above. But no sooner had Winchcombe acquired one school than another quickly followed. In 1621, Lady Frances Chandos arranged for a 'free grammar school' to be built in what is now Chandos Street. Since she had not visited the town for 30 years, she may not have realised that a new school had already been provided!

Anyway for a time the two establishements amalgamated though when in 1834 they divided, the master's annual salary was still, after two centuries, only £10. However, he could console himself with a fine flat and a marvellous view of the superb parish church.

IT is said that when the young bride came to live at Bishop's Cleeve Hall she so pined for her old home, that in one of the large rooms walls and ceilings were painted to remind her of what it looked like — over 150 years later it is still possible to identify Steanbridge House, Slad, both the Georgian front as well as Elizabethan back. There is also a lake with boat, and the drive shows the bridal carriage.

That we today can enjoy the scene is largely due to the restoration carried out 14 years ago when the agricultural firm Oldacres spared no effort to return this building to its former state. And what a worthwhile place it is. Dating from the 13th century, it has been described as the oldest and most splendid parsonage in Gloucestershire. My drawing shows the front facing that dangerous bend in the road, so that drivers may be less tempted to divert their attention to look at the real thing.

After all, Mistress Townsend had to be content with a picture of her Steanbridge House — though one hopes she came to love Cleeve Hall as much.

ONE of the Cotswolds' minor classics is the 'Diary of a Parson'. The Rev. Francis Witts recorded in some 90 notebooks daily events in his family, parish and county. This prolific output has been edited and published thus giving us an opportunity to savour life in the early 19th century.

My drawing of the Witts family home for more than 200 years shows the many additions to what was a 1680 parsonage. It also includes St. Peter's Church in the background, and rightly, because from 1808 to 1913 there was a Witts as rector. Today the parsonage has become an hotel; its name 'Lords of the Manor' is a reminder that in 1852 Mr. Witts bought the lordship of Upper Slaughter.

When we learn that he was also a magistrate, trustee manager of Stow Provident Bank, Chairman of Stow Board of Guardians, and committee member of the Turnpike Trust, it is not surprising he had plenty to write about in those notebooks!

THERE is the date 1613 over a doorway in a half-timbered cottage tucked away behind other houses in Stoke Orchard.

Why it should be called Old Rowley, the nickname of Charles II, is a mystery. Certainly the king didn't hide here after the Battle of Worcester, unless he made an unrecorded detour on 11 September, 1651 between Stow and Cirencester.

It is an intriguing cottage anyway, with original wattle and daub infills, and its more recent history is no less fascinating. One family here, the Suttons, manifested a zoological enthusiasm to the extent of having a snake in the inglenook; while another occupant was the pioneer flyer Amy Johnson who according to neighbours seemed quite a recluse — the milkman reported seeing merely a hand come round the door!

THE LESS familiar attractions of Painswick are the mills along the valley. Their names, from a past age of cloth and pin-making, include Lovedays, Skinners, Cap and Rock. But one is particularly interesting to musicians for the composer Gerald Finzi lived in the 17th century Kings Mill.

Attracted to Gloucestershire countryside and Painswick's gentle charm, it was here in 1922 that he composed his Violin Concerto, and appropriately the Severn Rhapsody. Though he never met that tragic son of Gloucester, Ivor Gurney, he championed his reputation, and ironically it was when he took another Gloucestershire composer, Vaughan Williams, up Church-down Hill during the 1956 Festival that he caught chicken pox from the Verger's child, and died from resulting complications.

Perhaps one day Painswick will put a plaque on Kings Mill House to record its illustrious resident, even if it was for only a few years.

MY DRAWING is of Mary Roberts' cottage, or to be more accurate, the cottage Mary Roberts lived in. For this is Whiteway where in 1898 ownership was a forbidden word. In that year, eight members from a Tolstoy Colony at Purleigh in Essex bought for £450 the 41 acres of Whiteway Farm near Miserden.

Their first act was to burn the deeds, and deny the necessity of money — though perhaps the £1,200 contributed by Samuel Thatcher, a Gloucester journalist, was not unwelcome. Anyway for a while this utopia enjoyed success, with "love the only law and goodwill the only guide". Then as human frailty showed itself friction developed: the leather worker found his trade conflicting with his vegetarianism, the baker preferred to run his business as a private enterprise, and sheer idleness was evident in the community. Samuel Thatcher tried to recover his money, another even took her claim to her house to the High Court, and others simply left.

Yet today even though there are new private houses at Whiteway, enough of the 80 original buildings remain to show what this bold experiment was like a century ago.

WHEN Horace Walpole visited Prinknash in 1774 he wrote: 'It stands on a glorious but impracticable hill in the midst of a little forest of beech, and commanding Elysium'. He was referring to the Old House which can be seen in front of the new monastery, and one wonders how many of the countless visitors who today come to Prinknash for the pottery or perfumery think of walking along the paths to see the former grange and hunting lodge of the abbots of Gloucester.

From 1514 Abbot Parker extended the house including such carvings as one of the young Henry VIII, together with the monograms of him and his first wife Katherine of Aragon. Such loyal gestures did not help much for in Parker's lifetime Henry destroyed the abbey at Gloucester and indeed Katherine soon was to be divorced.

In later years Prinknash Park became a private house, losing some of its treasures to places as varied as a museum in St. Louis and Gloucester Cathedral. But one thing cannot be taken away: its view, which King George III accounted 'the finest in my dominions'.

WHEN the words conservation or restoration are used we usually think of half-timbered houses, Georgian terraces and ancient churches. Yet there is another aspect just as rewarding and quite as urgent. Toddington, the subject of my drawing, illustrates it. Restoration has been going on here since 1981, not just with buildings important as they are, but also with machines and equipment.

The Gloucestershire Warwickshire Railway project has shown that enthusiasm, expertise and sheer hard work can produce stations, signal boxes, locomotives, coaches, all the glory of a past age from abandoned or forgotten sources.

The most conspicious feature in my drawing is the giant Hudswell Clarke Diesel Shunter made in Leeds in 1930. It was the first locomotive to arrive at Toddington for restoration; undoubtedly others will follow in its train as you might say.

THE ancient streets of Tewkesbury have a rich variety of buildings, mysterious alleys, and intriguing shop signs which can be seen above some of the facades. Among them is a padlock marking the business of Haywards. Back in 1820 George Hayward, a master cutter, started up three doors from the present shop, and when he died in 1859 his son continued as ironmonger, marrying the daughter of another similar tradesman.

Business flourished, so by 1900 the firm employed a blacksmith, tinsmith and whitesmith, making such varied items as iron seats and sheep troughs — their names incidentally were Ash, Birch and Twig! Today the Haywards still trade, though their catalogues offering bicycles at £6.10, treadle sewing machines for £5.17, and fifty four piece dinner services at £1.30 have long ceased. Thankfully another item has also disappeared — a 'humane man trap' priced from 90p to £1.09!

What has survived is the entrance to Malvern's or Post Office Alley which has the shop door at its street end.

THE ROAD from Cirencester to Bibury passes an octagonal lodge marking the entrance to Barnsley Park. Known as the Pepper Pot, it was built about 1800 to the designs of the great architect of London's Regent Park and Street, John Nash. But his is not the only famous name associated with Barnsley. Another is Sir Isaac Newton's. When he died in 1727, John Huggins of Fleet St. Prison bought his library for £300.

The 2,000 books eventually passed to his parson son who pasted his own bookplate in them, as in fact did the next owner James Musgrave. So when in 1920 some of the volumes were found at Barnsley they were at first unrecognised and many went to auction. Fortunately somebody realised whose they had been, consulted Musgrave's catalogue, and managed to rescue 860.

Today they are safely housed in Newton's old college at Cambridge, but Barnsley Park can proudly boast of once possessing part of one of the world's most historic libraries, and sharing a great scientist's work — even if it didn't know it!

WHEN visiting old churches we are accustomed to seeing the interior walls unadorned and chaste in their stonework or rendering. Yet in medieval times the impression would have been very different, and I know of no better way of showing this than suggesting a visit to the church at Hampnett near Northleach.

There its chancel is richly decorated, as it would have appeared in the Middle Ages. To be truthful it is the work of a Victorian rector but he was trying to recreate the original scheme of patterns.

It may not be to our modern taste, indeed Hampnett reminds me of an over-tattooed body, so if you do not like it there is still much delightful carving to enjoy, like the bobbing birds. And anyway, the hamlet itself is well worth visiting.

NOTHING it would seem could be more idyllic than life in a thatched cottage in a little Cotswold village. Well, here are some extracts from a bundle of letters discovered in the chimney of Rose Cottage, Oxenton:

'1824 July 11. To Miss E. Peart, Oxenton. Dear Girl, Sorry could not come on Sunday . . . am in hopes your child is not so cross . . . the scissors are for you . . . and the clasp is for to make you slender in the waist . . . let no one see these letters . . . P. Bramble.'

'1826 Jan. 31. My brother, Phillip Bramble, dangerously ill . . . anxious about you and the baby . . . if it lies in my brother's power he will send you something. Sarah Bramble.'

'1826 May 13. I cannot comply to send the little boy my [late] brother's fiddle as I wish to keep it. You have been wrongly informed about him being a married man . . . I send £2 which is all I can afford, and a smock for the child. S. Bramble.'

Perhaps not quite the blissful life after all?

CHIPPING Campden's long main street has a wealth of medieval buildings, among them the Woolstaplers Hall which houses a collection as rich and varied as the street itself. Built in 1340 for the Calf family whose symbol can be seen on a fireplace, five and a half centuries later it was owned by C. R. Ashbee who came to the town to start a Guild of Handicraft, and left his symbol in stained glass.

Both designs are easy to identify once you know the names they represent, but you may overlook them because of all the treasure that has been accumulating here since 1970. For Woolstaplers Hall is now a museum, one might say, of everything. There are kitchen items, cameras, typewriters, sewing machines, costume, scientific instruments — the list could go on. All are displayed without dull formality, so that it was indeed difficult to choose what to draw.

In the event I decided on the basket used by Lt. Lempriere for his balloon ascent over a century ago. But go along yourself and enjoy a collector's dream house. It has not really changed from the time they bargained for wool here.

FINE monuments in churches are always a pleasure to see, but sometimes they conceal a strange story. The memorial to the 1st Earl of Coventry in Elmley Castle church is an example of a family squabble which had an unexpected end.

For you should know that the noble Coventry ancestral church is at Croome in Worcestershire; yet the 1st Earl was denied a place there because his heir decided that the dowager Countess was the daughter of a commoner. However, the embarrassed widow saved the situation by remarrying, and her new husband, Thomas Savage, readily agreed to give space at his family church of Elmley Castle.

So that is why today you can enjoy the magnificent tomb showing the Earl proudly pointing to his coronet, and at the same time see only a few feet away one of the finest family memorials in Worcestershire, that of the Savages.

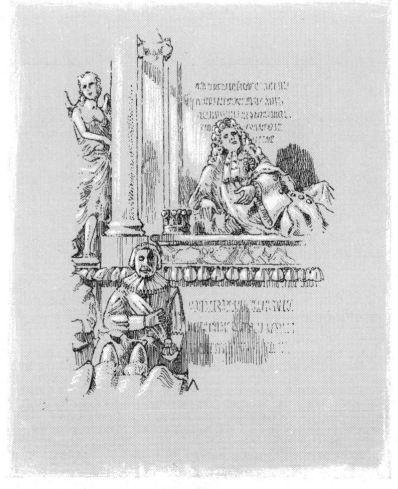

THE King's Head hotel in Cirencester market place leaves you in no doubt about its name for, as my drawing shows, keystone of doorway and window display it. Perhaps there might be a little uncertainty about the hotel's age since its front looks 19th century; but go inside and you will learn of a story that reaches back to 1340.

It has a history that includes high drama, for instance in 1688 when Lord Lovelace, on his way to join William of Orange's army, was captured in the hotel by the inappropriately named Captain Lorange. And there was bloodshed. Another example came 46 years earlier when Lord Chandos, arriving in the town to enlist support for Kings Charles I, was attacked by the pro-Parliament citizens, had his coach burnt and just escaped with his life by seeking refuge in the hotel. Again there was bloodshed, the first, it is said, of the Civil War.

How ironic that it should have been the King's Head; bearing in mind Charles I's fate on the scaffold!

TWO towers dominate a distant view of Prestbury — the church's and that forming part of a complicated building at the south end of the Burgage. The Lindens shows three styles superbly, with the 18th century's on the south side — the former Field House that was the vicar's home, then Miss Ashby's school for young ladies, and in 1843 a lodging for patients attending the hydropathic establishment of Morningside.

On the west is the Tower, whose origin is less clear, and perhaps most interesting of all, The Cottage whose half-timbering indicates a long history. For Linden Cottage was a farmhouse three centuries ago. Subsequent alterations and additions have produced intriguing walls and rooms, discoveries underfloor like straw and grain, even a Georgian golden guinea.

But most evocative of all are the numbers still to be seen on the medieval timbers, put there to ensure correct assembling. Who says pre-fabs are modern!

IF YOU are in Painswick and have keen eyes, you may notice a strange, battlemented building on a hillside to the south of the town. The curious will be tempted to make a journey across the valley to Bull's Cross for a closer look. It is said that this facade with its extraordinary windows was built by one of the Hyetts of Painswick House in the 18th century as a 'hate wall' to block the light to Greenhouse Court across the lane, for behind it was merely a lean-to barn or stables.

Further up the hillside there was once yet another strange building of Benjamin Hyett's bizarre invention — a mixture of Gothic and classical too, known as Pan's Lodge. Only the foundations remain, its purpose lost, though some say it was his hideaway for convivial parties out of reach of his wife.

Odd then that both buildings were painted conspicuously red. Maybe being at Bull's Cross had something to do with it!

THE church at Great Barrington is well worth visiting, if only for its setting next to the Georgian stables and remains of a Manor House which was the home of the Brays until Lord Chancellor Talbot bought it in 1735. Unfortunately he enjoyed it for less than a year before it was burned down. But the church stands as a reminder of those families. In the chancel is a memorial to Mary, Countess Talbot, widow of George III's Household Steward. It was carved by the great sculptor Nollekens, but another hand was responsible for the even more compelling monument near the entrance door.

This is by Christopher Cass and shows two of the Bray children being led over celestial clouds by a guardian angel. Jane died in 1711 of smallpox 'at her Aunt Catchmays in Gloucester,' while Edward died of the same disease in 1720 at the Royal Academy of Angiers, France. He was 15; she only eight years old.

If you look carefully you will find another Bray and you may wonder why his sword scabbard is on the wrong side. One story is that Captain Edmund Bray killed a man, and being pardoned at Tilbury by Queen Elizabeth I, resolved thereafter never to use his sword again.

Another explanation is that the sculptor found it more convenient to have the design this way, while others assert he was merely forgetful or careless. However, it is just possible of course that Edmund was in fact left-handed; I favour this theory myself, for I also am a 'southpaw.'

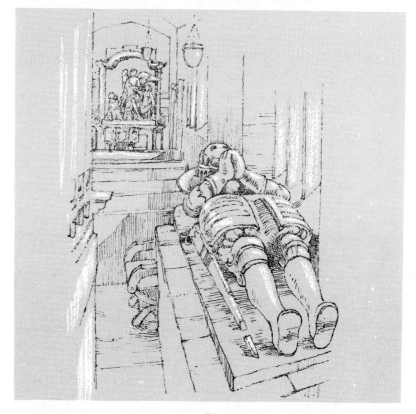

BUCKLAND near Broadway has the building shown in my drawing, probably the oldest continuously inhabited rectory in Gloucestershire. Its medieval past includes a hall used by the Abbot of Hailes. However, the stained glass is even more historic and intriguing. Not only are there the arms of St. Peter's Abbey, Gloucester, the badges of Edward IV, and a rector of 1466 but also something very unusual.

This subject represents the courtship dance of the blackcock, considered in medieval times a witch. The black and yellow birds hold in their beaks scrolls labelled 'In Jesu's name', probably to sanctify their activity. Some of the birds have been pierced by arrows, so perhaps here is the origin of 'Who Killed Cock Robin?' For remember he might not have been a redbreast but a robinet or witch's 'familiar'.

I wonder what John Wesley made of it all when he visited the Rectory?

MY drawing is of a cottage front door, or to be more precise of No. 88, Sherborne. Before you decide there has been some mix-up in the printing, I must state that the Norman stonework is quite authentic, having been removed from a 12th century church. Indeed, examine the cottage closely and more medieval doorways and windows will be discovered.

However, if you must find a mistake, then visit the present church by Sherborne House. In it you will see a memorial to Sir John Dutton where 'Peter' has been carved above the wrong name — and that by one of the greatest sculptors of the 18th century, Rysbrack!

YOU might suppose that Cotswold villages are pretty enough without the need to employ an architect. Yet this is what happened to Cornwell in 1938 when a wealthy American lady, discovering the place, commissioned Clough Williams-Ellis to make it picturesque. If you have visited Portmeirion in Wales you will have seen what he could create.

Well, here in Cornwell he gave the Manor House a breathtaking setting of terraces, water features, the school was transformed into a classical village hall, and cottages became almost like film sets. The only building he didn't touch was the Victorian vicarage.

Sadly, all this work had an unhappy ending for the American lady. She married an Englishman, Anthony Gillson, who was killed in the RAF during the last War. So in the event neither of them was destined to live in the Manor of Cornwell.

PARISH churches can be a rewarding place for the family historian, where not only local alliances are recorded on tombstone or tablet but also unexpected connections between the great and the good often appear. Such an example can be found at the church of St. John the Baptist, Wickhamford. Here as well as delightful box pews, three-decker pulpit and gigantic Royal Arms of Charles II, are the splendid double monuments in the chancel. These introduce us to the Sandys family whose relatives make impressive reading.

Sir Samuel and his son Sir Edward Sandys both died in 1626. They were related to Edwin Sandys, Archbishop of York in Elizabethan times, and Samuel through his second marriage to the widow of Henry Washington gained a stepdaughter whose great uncle was the grandfather of George Washington, 1st President of the U.S.A. Moreover, Henry who fought at the Battle of Worcester had a mother who was half-sister to George Villiers, Duke of Buckingham.

There, that should keep genealogists happy for a while at Wickhamford!

IT LOOKS an unusual building, that tower on the Oddington Road at Stow, but even more strange is the story of its creator, Richard Enoch. He had been in the East India Company and, so it was said, in Royal Service before Stow came to know of his eccentricities. A ship's figurehead of a Turk holding a dagger, a pillar and stone inscribed 'Enoch, the seventh from Adam' were but preliminaries to this tower and its museum.

What the contents were we may never fully know, but one exhibit has been recorded by the 'Illustrated London News'. On 22 September 1849 it stated that Mr. Enoch had harvested 1600 grains of wheat from a single grain which Mr. Chamberlayne of Maugersbury had given him. Even more extraordinary was the assertion that the original had come from a 2,400 year old mummy at Thebes.

Perhaps there was some leg-pulling, or maybe the 'curse of the Pharoahs,' for Enoch died nine years later — on September 22!

NORTHLEACH with its glorious church and houses of warm Cotswold stone is well suited to have a museum of countryside history. Yet fascinating as it is, quite as captivating, if such a term may be used, is the building that houses this museum — a prison.

Here in 1789 Sir George Onesiphorus Paul of Rodborough had his architect, William Blackburn, design a House of Correction that would treat prisoners humanely, give them exercise, allow them day and night cells, provide medical attention, and train them in crafts. No wonder his ideas were copied elsewhere in England and America, even if later they were diluted. Today, instead of young thieves and poachers there are some 25,000 willing visitors each year.

Nevertheless the past has not entirely disappeared, for the neighbouring wood still rejoices in the apposite name of Prison Copse!

THE ARTIST George Rowe, who played such a prominent part in the affairs of Cheltenham from 1832 to 1852, features in this series, but his wife deserves attention, too. Philippa was a pupil of his in Exeter, though she had been born many miles away in Spain's Seville, the daughter of an English soldier who died in battle on the day of her birth — as indeed did her mother on hearing the fateful news.

When George Rowe himself emigrated to Australia in the hope of restoring his fortunes, Philippa stayed behind to look after the family, supporting them by selling pictures she had painted. During this difficult period, she lived in several places. But the most interesting is undoubtedly Dutch Farm. It stands on the Shurdington Road, a fine 17th century house built by a merchant from the Netherlands, hence the name.

What a pity the inscription on its front has disappeared, for it so fitted Philippa's attitude to life: 'Neits zonder arbeit' (Nothing without labour). Come to think of it, George's philosophy was pretty much the same.